Praise for PORTRAITS OF THE SOUL

Anne is a bright guiding spiritual light. Alone with her would be enough, but here she offers a book of poetic inspiration - a connect to spirit.

Carell Ann Farmer, *Reiki Master, Visual Artist, Drum Carrier and Grandmother*

I'm very selective about the poetry I read. However, I found Dr. McMurtry's writing to be dramatically soul stirring. She is truly gifted in her ability to precisely capture your heart and mind as she writes with rich, energizing visuals that bring forward the deep truth of her words. Her connection with the Divine is evident, not only in her work in Reiki healing and with the crystal kingdom, but now brought forward in her writing. Dr. McMurtry's offering is a thought provoking and meaningful experience for the reader.

Barbara Halcrow, MSW, Author of *Ultimate Self-Care: A Holistic Guide for Strength and Balance in Changing Times* and *Spiritual Intelligence: How Your Spirit Can Lead You to Health, Happiness and Success*

Portraits of the Soul by Dr. Anne McMurtry is a delight for the heart and soul. Anne weaves sacred words with strong imagery and exquisite balance. Her collection of poems guides readers through a spiritual journey of depth and higher knowing. *Portraits of the Soul* becomes your friend along the way, providing inspiration and healing.

Dee Willock, Author of *Falling Into Easy: Help For Those Who Can't Meditate*

Dr. Anne McMurtry is not of this world. She sees beyond it to the other side, where the true being lives. When she looks into your eyes she knows what troubles you and why, thus offering you an insight into your own process and possibly a way to come to a resolution, hence freeing you from uncertainty. Anne's amazing book of poetry is inspired by some of the people whom she knows and some that she has worked with. Her poetry outlines some of their joys and their struggles and is infused with wisdom, hope and inspiration that can easily be adopted by anyone who reads her words as her messages are truly universal. *Portraits of the Soul* is a healing book and whoever reads its pages will experience acceptance and be embraced by the Divine and the Angels.

Devrah Laval, Author of *The Magic Doorway into the Divine* and *Leap to Freedom, Healing Quantum Guilt.*

Mother,
  You are a soul
with countless
gifts.. May this
book further
Stimulate your
own creativity.

Love
appreciation
  Anne

PORTRAITS OF THE SOUL

BY

DR. ANNE MCMURTRY

VANCOUVER, CANADA

Portraits of the Soul © 2020, Dr. Anne McMurtry

ISBN: 978-1-7770835-0-2
Cover design: Diane Feught

Dr. Anne McMurtry
geminimcmurtry@gmail.com

*Dedicated to all those souls whose spirit
ignites our courage and lights up our path.*

CONTENTS

— DR. ANNE MCMURTRY —

Portraits of the Soul

FOREWORD

When, after a several years of no contact, my having moved away from the Lower Mainland, Anne called me up in July of 2019 to ask me for some editorial assistance in putting together *Portraits of the Soul*, my answer was an immediate "yes."

I'd known Anne for over 20 years and had come to know her more deeply after the suicide of my brother, Steve, in 2004. When I went to her with my shredded heart, she not only provided me with comfort, she also bestowed me with the spiritual wisdom I needed to help myself – and my brother – through that difficult passage. In her capacity as a channel, she knew personal details about Steve, despite never having met him or even having heard about him prior to his death, that could only have come from having made a genuine connection with him in the spirit world.

A friend asked me recently if Anne was "the real deal" as a spiritual teacher. My answer was an immediate "yes" then as well. Not because Anne's a saint. She's as mortal as the rest of us and is not afraid to share her all-too-human struggles and challenges.

But she is also not afraid to convey her enduring love for Spirit. When it comes to her love for the Divine, Anne makes no attempt to play it cool. It is a love that I and many others who have benefitted from her readings and healing sessions have learned to count on.

It is this all-encompassing, unconditional love that distinguishes this remarkable collection of sacred poetry. In every one of

— DR. ANNE MCMURTRY —

these poems, Anne shares her love for those who inspired them, for the spiritual impulse that informed them, and for the readers who need them. Readers who need a generous infusion of love to guide them and to anchor them in these times of great turmoil and uncertainty.

This love is not sentimental, kittens-and-unicorns love. It is a love that has been hewn from having lived wholeheartedly through times of suffering and grace. As she says in her poem, *Against the Ascetic*:

>I must drink from my tears
>And build with my burdens
>For my wings were fashioned
>>from the shadows

Hers is a love that is indelible, having emerged from the realization that this Earth life is a precious gift.

It is also accompanied by a high degree of spiritual knowledge and intelligence. Universal in her spirituality, Anne hasn't just studied the sacred texts for all major faiths; she has lived them. They're not merely reference books to her; they're beloved companions. The poems on these pages were inspired by Anne's love for the ancient teachings and, in their fulfillment, they are touchstones for the spiritual journey. Although often focused on the soul signature of a particular individual, the poems are meant for all of us as they gently and powerfully point the way to our unique spiritual pathway.

Donaleen Saul
Author, *Did You Know I Would Miss You? The Transformational Journey of the Suicide Survivor*

Prologue

"Works of art are of an infinite loneliness and with nothing so little to be reached as with criticism. Only love can grasp and hold and be just toward them." - Rainer Maria Rilke, *Letters to a Young Poet*

How these poems came into being is an eternal mystery to me. I never sat down with the intention of writing any of them. The first few lines would come to me and I would be given the choice by Spirit of working with the material or not.

I have frequently wondered if I was perhaps communicating with the guardian angels of the people who inspired them. The poems are not so much a portrait of their personality, nor of their conventional sense of themselves, but of their essence. Because of that, they have often opened up new areas of self-discovery for their subjects.

When I perform one of these poems in public, it is not uncommon for a member of the audience to come up to me and say, "It seemed as though you were talking directly to me!" Although the poem was about someone else, they felt as though I was inside their own experience. This is another mystery!

— Dr. Anne McMurtry —

The beginnings of a poem can arrive in that liminal space between sleep and waking, in meditation, or even out on my bicycle doing my daily errands. I have gotten into the habit of having a notebook and pen with me, wherever I am.

Sometimes the death of someone I love, or even of someone I have never met, will inspire a poem. Because the essence of these poems has been given to me by Spirit, I have felt the need to pass them on. Many years ago, I made an agreement with Spirit to publish them, an agreement that I am now honouring.

It is my intention that whoever reads these poems will experience a deeper sense of themselves and of the profound connection we all share with Spirit.

To quote Thomas Merton, one of my favourite Christian mystics, "My dear brothers and sisters, we are already one. But we imagine that we are not. So what we have to recover is our original unity. What we have to be is what we are."

I

FAMILY

Families are like branches on a tree.
We grow in different directions yet our roots remain as one.

- UNKNOWN

Dad

He was a friend to everyone
and a helping hand to every lost soul
yet he often saw himself as lost
Because he did not see
the brilliance and depth
of his own heart
and the multitudinous ways
that God was using him
to bring peace
to many troubled souls.

I hope now that he knows
the love that he kindled
in so many hearts
that keeps blazing even now
in his physical absence

Truly God showered His Love upon us
by sending us this shepherd.

MOTHER: AN APPRECIATION

If God had given you a chance
to have one wish fulfilled
you would have asked that all of your children
and all of your loved ones
would find true happiness
and have the chance to realize
their deepest dreams.

That was your request.

Then you thought
if that is not possible
I will nurture them with the best food
and loving care
and truly encourage them
when they seem to have lost their way.

Just as you offered Jill
your first-born
your whole heart and soul
when she was dying
your best joy
always came
from serving others.

— DR. ANNE MCMURTRY —

MY SISTER JILL

She often experienced her Spirit
as too large for her body
and even for the confines
of her personality

And every so often it would spill out
suddenly
like a flash of lightening
or a bolt of thunder

For she was always traveling
Between two dimensions
And sometimes, like Alice in Wonderland
she would get lost trying to find her way back.

So her exuberance and her joy,
though it always celebrated
the beauty of this earth
and all that we can experience here.
came from another dimension

so often in the most difficult situations
she was strangely lighthearted like the fairies
yet fearless like the angels

perhaps her mission was to shower us
with a whole other frequency
of Light and Courage
to show us how to be
passionately present
in each moment.

Peter

You are like someone who is bilingual
You are equally schooled
in the language of the head
and the language of the heart.

The language of the head schools you
In the ways of the world
with its inevitable rollercoaster ride
of success and failure
approval and disapproval

But the language of the heart schools you
in the ways of love
which lead you into the healing power
of kindness and compassion
And finally into the most sublime Joy
The Sacred Heart of God.

— Dr. Anne McMurtry —

SUSAN

It has been said
"Love is that tension toward the particular"
That ability to learn exactly what is needed
by each soul in each moment

Your angels have trained you
in this sacred science
You are a soul
Who exudes unconditional love
the energy that allows every soul to blossom
This enables you to listen
with total attention and an open heart.

Your greatest challenge
Is to allow yourself to receive
what you so generously give to others
For God truly wants you to bathe in the Radiance
of your own heart.

Lucy

Like Mary pregnant with the Christ Child
your being is pregnant with a new frequency of consciousness
that allows you to see and experience everything
with the crystal clarity of the soul

But you are still trying to give form to
a language for this seeing
Your poetry and music point to it
But often something unexpressed
gnaws at you
and pushes you to new levels
of self-expression

For you do realize
that a certain level of discernment
is necessary
and that part of being an artist and spiritual seeker
is living in many dimensions at one time

Allow yourself to be held
by all those unseen Presences
of Love and Light
Your sacred midwives
who will always mirror and protect
the clear vision and power
that you have been given.

— Dr. Anne McMurtry —

Sarah

Picture a meadow filled with every wild flower
and every exotic bird and butterfly
And you get a sense of the splendor of this soul
who exudes such appreciation
for the sacred beauty of this Earth.

Her gentleness and warmth
create such a sense of safety
and her medicine of listening
heals many a troubled heart

She knows that Peace
is the most potent power
and whatever robs us of that Peace
is not worth reaching for.

My Grandfather

You were the first soul to teach me
that life is not as it appears
that it is only when we open our hearts
that life begins to flower.

You always experienced God
not as the judge that condemns us
but as the loving Friend
Who always walks with us
And as the Beloved
Who beckons us into a life of sacred service.

The light from your awakened heart
was so brilliant
It continues to illumine my path
and to deepen my resolve
even now
even after all these years.

— Dr. Anne McMurtry —

My Grandmother

You saw the earth as only a lover would
As the Beloved
who showed you a different face every moment
whose beauty often intoxicated you
and certainly made your heart sing

you never saw the need for religious ritual or lengthy prayers
"Nature is the most sacred temple," you would say,
"Worship God there."

For he has inscribed His signature
within every being

"Beauty and Truth walk hand in hand," you would say
"Truth must be eloquent
It must have colour and harmony
and emit a haunting fragrance
Before it can capture our hearts."

NANCY

Like the nectar of the honeycomb,
when Nancy holds you in her heart
she creates a real sweetness
that lingers like the rarest perfume.
Because of the warmth of her heart,
she can inspire
a feeling of safety
in even the most frightened soul.

She would say it is a privilege
to pray for any souls that are suffering
as she wants to share
the Loving Presence of the Christ
that walks with her.

My prayer for you, Nancy,
is that you will catch a reflection
of your own most sacred heart
and like the cat basking in a pool of sunlight
you too will bask in the purity and power
of the Great Light within you.

— Dr. Anne McMurtry —

Margaret-Ann

It seems as if you did not have time to finish your story
And a passionate story it was
About the history of mankind
And the unique history of your extended family

But perhaps Spirit wanted you to focus
on the most special history of all

The history of your own soul
which I know you are seeing now
flashing before you
like the most sacred revelation.

I hope now you are appreciating
The immense colour and generosity of your spirit
As you see the sparks of light and love
That you passed on to so many.

You were such a great teacher
Because you always celebrated
The wisdom in all of us

And like a true midwife
You helped to birth
The Epiphany of many a soul.

Upon My Sister's Death

This cry
kills
every shield of thought
every dance of wit and word
Every blind of brain and heart

It is the first and the last cry
The cry for light
And the cry for rest

The rage of love
        From the chase of death

The lance of time
        Into the dreams of dust

It is not a cry for children
Though they hear it best
For them, words are still strangers
And not to be trusted.
One cry
And after much hiding
The last cry
And then...

— Dr. Anne McMurtry —

MY MOTHER'S PIETÀ

Like the measureless pain of Mother Mary
who carried the Crucifixion within her aching heart,

so you carried the pain
of your daughter's death
until you could bear it no longer

And at the hour of your death
The Christ in His tender mercy
Carried you into the arms of
The Infinitely Loving Father
where you found
all whom you had loved
all whom you thought you'd lost
And you saw in amazement that they had never left you.

So all whom you loved on Earth
may grieve your physical absence
But we know
Your heart is always with us
For where there is Love
There is no separation.

My Mother's Passing into Light

She was always pregnant
With a force of Love
Infinitely larger than even her most loving actions
Love would spill out now and then
Like hot lava
Whenever she let go of form
and simply surrendered

But she could only birth it fully
when she was passing over
when Life and Death intersected
within the Infinity of God's Heart

Then the full force of her love
Erupted like a flaming volcano
Showering us all
with the sacred flames
of her courageous and generous heart.

— Dr. Anne McMurtry —

2

SOUL MATES

Let me not to the marriage of true minds admit impediments.
Love is not love which alters when it alteration finds,
or bends with the remover to remove.
O no! it is an ever-fixed mark
That looks on tempests and is never shaken.

- Sonnet 116, WILLIAM SHAKESPEARE

JULIA

You are
that brilliant rose
whose petals pervade
the beauty of this earth
whose fragrance fills my heart
with an unbounded joy.

To touch you in any form
is to feel the pulsation of that Force
that fills every being
with light and aliveness

Even your eyes
radiate the pulsation
of the sun
as your hands hold
the soothing balm of the moon
like nectar from the night sky

Like the first plane
that broke the sound barrier
your being breaks through
every boundary
and every limitation
to birth a space of Being
like the flight of the eagle
like the cry of the soul
as it lifts up
from this emerald sphere
we call earth
to soar back to that Sacred Source
We call Home.

FOREVER FRIENDS (TO KATHY)

I see two little girls
playing together in a rose garden
where the birds never stop singing
and the butterflies keep returning.

We have always known each other
and will always find our way
back to this garden
and back to this connection.

even when life appears to rob us of the taste of joy
and the full flavor of love.

Trust is a treasure that cannot be measured.
It is a jewel of inestimable value.

Whatever happens in our journey together
The trust is always there
Its foundation was laid lifetimes ago.

We have been sisters, friends, mothers, daughters, monks
and we know that whatever the form
if love is not present
life is not possible.

— DR. ANNE MCMURTRY —

Bernice

Some angels assume
the appearance of a human body
in order not to alarm us
or to draw attention to themselves.

But every so often
I cannot fail to see the brilliance
of your Light
shining like a star in all directions
and I feel your infinite longing
to return to the Source of that Light
when your task is complete.

But I realize
you have taken that most sacred vow
the Bodhisattva vow
that postpones that return
until all souls have been delivered from their suffering
and the earth is once again filled with Light

"God is my food and drink,"
you tell me,
"and my oasis in the desert.
I will never be alone or without a light
Even in the deepest darkness."

I smile as I leave you
Knowing that God is grateful
He has such a beloved friend.

GAIL

Even in your human frailty
you were such a warrior
and such a loving teacher

Reminding us
that just as the trees shed their leaves
in the fall
so shall we shed our human costume

But when our soul hears its call
that which we truly are
keeps springing back
again and again
like the sun that rises every morning.

You were such a living paradox
housing such unlimited power
and unlimited compassion
within the disguise of your all too human form.
for every soul found its reflection
in your immense heart.

But it is as a lover of the earth
that you will be most remembered
for you loved her
with such a fierce tenderness
and a constant devotion

And I can feel her sadness and gratitude
both blending now
as she blesses you with a vast rainbow
that encircles the earth
as you pass now
into That Infinite Light

— Dr. Anne McMurtry —

WE ARE ONE

I come to you hungry and you show me
My own fullness

I come to you broken and you show me
My wholeness

Is your love
A part of me I lost centuries ago?
A jewel of light lost somewhere in the labyrinth of time?

Can your love be that ancient navigator
That will lead me Home?

Silence Tastes of You

Silence tastes of you
like the mute reach of eyes
or the shy language of hands

But you have long been gone
Into a land I know not

Yet I still hear you

Love

In the sudden thrust
Of quiet things

— Dr. Anne McMurtry —

Your Hands Hold the Key

Your hands hold the key to my every emotion
And to every hidden place of my heart.

When you touch me,
I feel myself exploding into being
Awakening suddenly from a long sleep.

For your love is like a midwife
Drawing me out, ever so gently
yet ever so firmly
Into the Light.

You teach me, not with words
But with the constant miracle of your touch
That we are being born newly every moment
Into this rich banquet of beauty
That is almost more than enough.

ALL THIS LEAVES A SCAR

The hunger of wind and sky
The flood of calm in the pale space on night
Trees burnt against a dying sun

All this leaves a scar.

Which I touch on the lines of your face
Some mumble old prayers
You offer your tears

At dusk, I find them
Scattered like pearls
On the face of each leaf.

— DR. ANNE MCMURTRY —

Is Love Ever Lost?

Even when the doors are locked between us
padlocked with layers of anger and blame
I am surprised by how much Light
insists on flowing through
and with such sweet extravagance

Like Mary Magdalene
pouring sacred oils on Christ's feet
without measure
without limit

The soul never stops loving
any more than the sun stops shining
despite the rain clouds of the ego
and the armour of the will

We think it is the human Other we are seeking
But look again
See what is hidden in every human heart
that longs to be revealed
The Love that loves us
Without condition
Without end

3

FRIENDS

*The day, if it ever comes, when you are given true affection,
there will be no opposition between interior solitude and friendship,
quite the reverse.*

- SIMONE WEIL

Joy

Who will look after the little ones?
The children who have been abandoned?
The animals that have been abused?
The hearts that have been shattered?

So God sent us the soul known as Joy
Who brings with her the fragrance
of the Divine Mother
Who champions all her loved ones
with a fierce devotion
a tender protection

Isn't it time
that Joy received the sacred boomerang
of all that she has given
so that she may abide
in the grace and fullness
of her own heart
while on this sacred assignment?

Rae

Picture a rainbow
exploding into a number of musical notes
Picture the blue firmament
of the sky
becoming a myriad of shooting stars

And you get a sense of the infinite range
of this soul
Not only musically,
where she is especially gifted
But most importantly,
as a human being
and as a soul.

For she can be downright earthy one moment
and soaring with the angels the next

She can be wading through seas of sorrow one moment
and exuding the most exquisite ecstasy the next.

For she never likes to limit herself to any emotion
or any dimension
Rather she embraces the whole kaleidoscope of life
with equal passion

She is truly a soul
who keeps reaching for the highest possibility
in every moment.

— Dr. Anne McMurtry —

Donaleen: The Soul Who Dives into the Depths

Reading about the mystics is one thing
Meeting one in the flesh is quite another.

This soul walks and talks
with all the lovers of God.

Most of God's friends are very humble
and she is no exception
But she can bring you into the fire
of God's presence
with just a glance
with just an intention
Especially when she blasts you
With the full force of her heart.

Like every soul that is truly on a mission
she realizes it is her job
to simplify the sacred teachings,
and to direct us to the sacred Teacher within.

But what she wants above all
is to have every soul
who comes across her path
to be initiated into the Sacred Heart of God
and to know no fear.

STEVE

When you decide to love someone
your heart is steady
like an ancient compass
or like Ram
when he was taken from his beloved Sita
and never lost heart.

Knowing that God's will
always delivers us when the time is right
You don't merely dream

You steadily build the temple
that God intended
You offer your selfless service
like the rose offers its nectar
to the wind

Even in the hardest of times
you never give up.

— Dr. Anne McMurtry —

Zo-ey

You are a sensitive and refined instrument
Like a concert violin tuned by a Master
You can produce the most exquisite music
Not only the music heard by the ear
But the music heard by the soul
emitted into the ethers
like a sacred fragrance
where every level of our being
opens like a Rose
to the power of Divine Light

Your being embodies the power of gentleness
which can open even the most stubborn heart
like the harp used by David
that soothed even the anger of Goliath
you heal not only with your hands
but also with your intention
you always intend the highest outcome
in any situation

Truly you are one of God's most beloved friends.

REUBEN

As a teacher who kindles
the love of learning in his students
and opens them to the full adventure
Life can be.
When he drums, he dissolves
into the sound itself
which expands and expands
into the very pulse of The Universe
into the most sacred heartbeat of Shiva.

How strange and exhilarating
that we are most truly ourselves
when we step out of ourselves
into something infinitely immense
and realize
that Who We Really Are
Only God knows.

— DR. ANNE MCMURTRY —

Cuba

It can be said that God feels the most exquisite pain
when we turn away from Him
and choose the mirage of our own making
rather than the miracle
that comes from surrender.

You are a soul
who has always been willing
to dive into the depths and retrieve lost souls,
like Christ finding the sheep that have strayed from the fold.

Truly you know it is a sacred commandment
That we must carry each other's burdens
But you do it so lightly
As if it were the sweetest gift.

Perhaps that is because you know only too well
what it is to feel lost
and what it is
to choose again
To choose Light
And Love and Mercy.

YASMIN

You are a very special archangel
That brings a special power into this dimension
that takes just a little getting used to.

Even your most casual comment
pierces through all the ego's defences
and unveils the soul.

You realize that even God
has a tight schedule
and we have no time to lose.

"Now is the time to wake up
Not tomorrow," you would say

So you continually offer your love and your wisdom
To support this awakening
And to banish every fear.

"We can't wake up alone,"
you would say,
"Love and only Love brings us to that final frontier."

— Dr. Anne McMurtry —

Lori: A Beacon for All of Us

Like the endless love of God
her heart was a pool of compassion
for every creature

For her finest jewels were not her crystals
though she had many
but all the four-legged creatures
that had crept into her heart.
Their love lit up her path like countless lanterns
or like the stars that light up the night.

Whatever creature was fortunate enough
to be loved by her
human or otherwise
found that her love was steady and sure
like a compass

And like the boundless depths of the ocean
it defied all limits.

Truly her soul was a beacon of light
a flame of boundless enthusiasm
a force of Divine Love
that will continue to burn brightly
Wherever she is.

To the Lipsett Family

I notice that your words weave in and out
of a Vast Silence
like trees etched against an open sky
like wild flowers scattered on an empty grave
Even within the richness of your caring
there is always room for Spirit to speak

Your hearts remind me that we must be
still before we can speak
that we must separate
before we can come together
that we must Be, fully
before we can love.

— Dr. Anne McMurtry —

Gina's Gift to Us All

Just as Christ continued to carry us all
                              in His immense heart
Even while he was dying
So Gina insisted on carrying
                              every broken and bruised soul
Within her immense heart.

Strangely enough,
as her own wounds grew deeper,
her courage and compassion
expanded even more.

For she knew with absolute certainty
That only the purest,
                              most unconditional love
could antidote personal pain and suffering.

In the end,
her surrender to That Love
has lit up her heart
                              with all the colours of the angels
                              and all the fragrance of the saints

So that Light pours through her constantly
Like sunlight streaming through
A sacred stained glass window

She has always walked with God
So with great gratitude
For the gift she has been
                              to all of us
We commend her now
Into God's Infinite Care.

4

HEALERS AND TEACHERS

*Healers and teachers are merely awakening
what is already within each soul.*

- DR. ANNE MCMURTRY

CARELL

Your being is a delicate but very precise instrument
that vibrates to the frequency
of the angelic realm
for you have been imprinted
with their sacred geometries of light and healing.

Your heart has always been wedded to God
so your being exudes a fragrance
that naturally awakens in others
their thirst for truth
and their hunger for goodness

Because a part of you resides in the highest realm,
You know the ripple effect
of all of our actions and thoughts
So you try to choose only those that will benefit
all sentient beings.

Truly you are a soul with a dual citizenship
A beloved citizen of this realm of name and form
But especially loved in that realm
where only Light and Love can survive.

DEBBIE'S DARSHAN

She carries you in her heart with such safety
like the kangaroo carries its young
yet she can be fierce
like a mother bear with its cubs
when she senses you are in danger

"I am not doing anything," she says,
"All this is the dance of the Shakti
It is your own inner Self
that is carrying you
and will never drop you
even in the heaviest moment."

But I say:
"Your love is like a diamond
that cuts through any darkness
and like the lightning of the Guru's Glance
dissolves any despair
for you are that sacred bridge
that continues to carry countless souls
from this vale of tears
to the splendor of Light awaiting us on the other side."

— DR. ANNE MCMURTRY —

BERNICE'S BLESSING

Your hospice work is not simply
to hold the hand of the dying
though that angelic assignment
dispenses countless sacred blessings.

It is even more extensive
as you hold the hearts of the many
Who have forgotten why they are living
crushed as they are by the unending torment of pain

You help each soul connect with the Great Design
that God has for each of us
whether on this plane of Being
or the next

Your soul knows that
Only unconditional Love will resurrect
all the broken spirits,
Bringing them back to that sacred space
in God's Heart
where they remember
Who they truly are.

SHANTI

I see Shiva and Shakti
moving playfully
and sometimes even passionately
amongst your words
which often sparkle
with a Light
beyond this dimension
and amongst your movements
which often resemble a flowing river

For your energy is often too large
for your body
and spills over
becoming flashes of light
and sparkles of energy

For you see the kundalini
stretching us to be all that we can be
cutting away at our limitations
like a loving laser.

— DR. ANNE MCMURTRY —

PAULINE

Your face is often surrounded
by such a brightness
I often wonder
if your human face isn't just a disguise
for an infinitely loving Presence

for your eyes blaze with the fiery flames
of the seraphim
and reach into every dimension
and your heart always inspires such fearlessness
in the souls you are holding

For you are one of those brave souls
who is truly a trail-blazer
willing to dive into dark and unknown depths
to unveil the treasure within.

Did God ask you then,
to come into this darkened planet
to plant a luminous Rose
into the center of our hearts?

so that we could find our way
out of the labyrinth of this world
back to the Source of Light itself?

FAREWELL TO AN ANGEL
(in remembrance of Ann Fleming)

Because she always knew she was not
that costume we call the body
or that limited container
we call the personality
She lived ecstatically
like an exclamation mark
without apology
and without defence.

Ignited from within
with a real passion for truth
that laughed at every apparent limitation
and easily extinguished every passing doubt.

Yet the strongest force that flowed from her heart
was her boundless compassion
and limitless love

For the strongest souls
are often infinitely tender.

Like a true shaman
she died as she lived
without any hesitation
Even in that moment,
confronting the darkness with blazing light
fearless and free

A warrior of the heart,
she will never be forgotten.

— DR. ANNE MCMURTRY —

THE GATHERING
(inspired by the chanting of Guru Raj Kaur Khalsa)

Like countless fireflies we gather
to light up the night
with our circle of fire
and to find our way Home

Young and old, rich and poor
Our faith has many faces
but comes
From That Single Source
That Nameless Light
that holds the night together

For in every heart that is free of fear
there burns a steady flame
that can light up the whole world
All it takes to light the Sacred Fire
is a single match

Are you ready?

WHAT CHRIST HAS TAUGHT YOU
(for Cuba)

Christ was a skilful counselor
He knew when to speak
And when to be silent
So when Mary Magdalene gave way to despair
at the empty Tomb
He listened to her with total attention
until she could see
she was not speaking to the gardener
but to the Risen Lord

So Christ has taught you how to heal others
by directing the purest attention
into their deepest wound
at times using the medicine of Silence
at other times the medicine of Right Speech
that cuts through delusion and doubt
like arrows of light

You always demonstrated
That life only works when we follow His commandment
and cast our burdens upon His shoulders
and carry that yoke together
with faith and lightness of heart.

— DR. ANNE MCMURTRY —

Who is the Healer?

Who is the healer?
Someone who has been broken
Again and again
but has still chosen
Love over Fear
Trust over Mistrust

And like a magnet
This simple choice draws in
The radiance of the angels
The steady clear flame of the Masters
who then use this simple soul
to bring a little light into the darkness
And to be that bridge, however frail,
over the troubled waters of this life

As Lao-tse said,
"The journey of a thousand miles begins with one step."
The step of trust over mistrust.

CHRIS GRISCOMBE: THE MEDICINE OF YOUR HEART

Like that coat of many colours
Like that sudden shower of stars
Your Light bursts through the veil
revealing all those hidden worlds
that stream forth from your eyes
Like a constant fountain of Love

You stand in the power
of that Sacred Fire
before which even the seraphs shudder
You wield its crystal sword
like a true warrior of Spirit

But I most love the child in you
who shows me my own Infinity
and the dance that leads us back
into the very Heart of God.

— DR. ANNE McMURTRY —

PAMELA'S DARSHAN

The true lover of God
does not want to dance on the surface
She wants to dive into the very heart of Love
until every distinction between lover and Beloved
is dissolved.

So the deepest gift of devotion
Is not a prolonged practice of prayer
But a letting go of the very notion of "I"
Until this whole illusion of duality
manifesting as "you" or "me"
is revealed as God's playful Dance.

THE HEARTSONG OF MATTIE STEPANEK

Sent from the Unseen Realms
This little ambassador of Peace
This angelic messenger
chose a body that could only operate
within a shroud of pain

Yet his purpose was always to embody
Joy and Light
For such an Infinity of Love constantly
poured out of his fragile and finite vessel
Like every angel
He pointed out that Peace must be consciously chosen
And practiced daily

I know his spirit would simply
want us all without exception
to dive into our hearts,
to find the song that is buried there
and to sing it with an honest passion

Sometimes all it takes
is for one soul to fully embody Peace
and the world is never the same again.

— DR. ANNE McMURTRY —

Borges: The Inner Traveller

Borges didn't merely write poems and stories
He provided us with metaphysical maps
that unlock the secret chambers
of the Inner World
allowing us entry into spaces of numinous power

He was an explorer and an adventurer
who reached into some of the last wildernesses
of mind and imagination

as with Milton and Homer
perhaps his blindness provided him access
to all those inner worlds
that allowed him to see
As the soul sees.

TERRY FOX

His battle with cancer didn't break his spirit
It fueled his determination
to rise up like the phoenix from the ashes
To truly impart
A vision of transcendence
Where anything is possible
for the soul that is ruthlessly obedient
to the Divine Command

Like an arrow traveling toward its target
He never deviated from his goal
even to savour the most innocent distraction

Not realizing until the end
That his target would be just
on the other side of this thin veil.

For when one soul truly surrenders
To God's Will
That soul becomes a sacred lever
that lifts up and releases even the heaviest weight of this world
allowing the most brilliant light
to pour in
without measure.

It might be said that his quiet spirit
started a revolution that even he could not foresee
that will continue to break down complacency
and root out despair
Kindling that flame of steady courage in countless souls.

Like the great eagle
His spirit watches over us as we take up his torch
and run with it
Until all souls battling with this disease
are truly free.

— DR. ANNE MCMURTRY —

5

FELLOW TRAVELLERS

*The traveller has to knock on every alien door to come to his own,
and one has to wander through all the outer worlds
to reach the innermost shrine at the end.*

- RABINDRANATH TAGORE

RON

There was such strength
in his gentleness
and courage
                    in his playfulness
For he always knew
the great trial
that was coming.

Perhaps because
He always felt
The Love
At the heart of things
He could laugh
Even when facing his worst fear.

But in his
seeming simplicity
there was
a great wisdom
Even Shakespeare knew
That the clown
Could see through the veil
and was
Not caught
In the web of desire.

May the greatest souls
Travel with him now
As he journeys
Beyond all name
and form
Into that
Great Flame of Love
That alone is.

THE LION-HEARTED
(for Eileen)

Like the lion
You thrive on wildness
(and sometimes even a sweet fury)
allowing only the wind to comb your mane
and brush against your face

Rain and Thunder
They are more friends to you than enemies
Fellow rebels against complacency
"Umbrellas are surely for cowards," you would say

Yet if the lion was not looking for the wizard
knowing that all wizardry is within
was it not looking for courage
the courage perhaps to roar
and no longer to whisper?

But you have always known
That the Light alone has courage
and is endlessly patient

— DR. ANNE MCMURTRY —

BRYAN

When God measures our strength
it is often the reverse of our human measurements

For what we call strength
God sees as weakness
And what we call weakness
God sees as strength.

Christ embraced the paradox
that the meek, not the self-assured and proud,
shall inherit the earth
And only those souls who do not walk in the world's shoes,
The pure in heart
Shall see God.

Bryan, did you not know
that your life,
especially your heart,
embodies these teachings?
And that your being itself
embraces the beatitudes?

Allow yourself then to be showered
by God's countless blessings
to be held by all his angels
and to know that you are infinitely loved
In this realm and in the next.

ANN

Married to God
Obedient to His Will
She moves in and out of people's lives
lightly
like a butterfly
showering beauty and kindness
wherever she goes

Like a true angel
She resists no sacred assignment
but performs even the most difficult task
with ease and grace

Isn't it time for her to see the light that she is?
and the myriad seeds of grace
she has implanted in so many souls?

For when all the veils around the soul have been removed
She will finally sense that Presence of Peace
that walked with her
every step of the way.

— DR. ANNE MCMURTRY —

EMILY

At war with her own beauty
and ill at ease with the Shakti
spinning through her body

she tries to find a way
through everyone else's absolutes
to a truth that is uniquely her own.

Beneath her apparent rebellion
there is a vast awareness and compassion
that leaks out

despite her attempts to keep everything in.

ALEX

He is not quite sure
if he is an alien
or a human
but he possesses a vast intelligence
that like a new and very advanced machine
he is still learning to operate

and despite the protocol that says
"men should not be sensitive"
his heart feels very deeply
which his eyes reveal
behind even the heaviest sunglasses.

— DR. ANNE MCMURTRY —

SUNNY-B

His little body cannot possibly contain
the enormous joy and aliveness
that his spirit exudes
for every part of his life is an exclamation mark!

Nothing is done or felt halfway.

So his gift to all of us
is to break us away
from all our little prisons
and to take us to a place
that is truly free
and full of joy.

COLETTE

Like the dervish
whose head tilts to one side
as he twirls in ecstasy
around an invisible sacred point
so your head tilts to one side
when you chant God's name
as if you too were whirling in ecstasy

You perform so many duties
with a consistent, unwavering
Joy

For you experience Shiva dancing through you.
not only when you are chanting or in deep meditation
but also in the most everyday tasks.
"The splendour and the simplicity are one,"
you would say,
"It's all part of the sacred design."

— DR. ANNE MCMURTRY —

LYLE

Like the very nature of the blue pearl
that in one moment reveals itself
as the tiniest seed
and in the next, the cosmic energy
beyond all time and form

So your power shows itself in one moment
as an impish grin
that takes in the whole situation in a glance
but in the next moment
you are the genius who creates statues
of enduring grace and beauty

You understand that real power
is both playful and majestic

We never quite know
which face will reveal itself first
For the ways of the Shakti
are always veiled in Sacred Mystery.

JIAN

When I admitted to her
that I loved sunsets
the way some people love wine or chocolate
a barrier fell away
a window suddenly opened
to reveal a common love of beauty
that dissolved the usual distinction
between doctor and patient
and unveiled the true humanity
we all share at the core
the common yearning for meaning and beauty
and the kindness that still lives in the heart
despite every disappointment

— DR. ANNE MCMURTRY —

COLIN

Moses initially resisted God's calling
He felt unworthy

So when Bliss pursues you
you perceive it as a case of mistaken identity
like the deer that seeks the musk outside of itself
not knowing its own fragrance.

But now it is time for you to stop
running from this Bliss
to bathe in the radiance
of your own being
and to truly know
your own divinity.

BEATRICE

There are many ways back to Centre
each with its own depth and hue.
The way that is right for you
must fit snugly like a shoe so comfortable
you don't even know you have it on.

The most sacred path
you would say
is one where we are totally true
to the Master and Teacher within us
And you would want to celebrate
This Awakening with all the sacred arts
as you experience the Divine
Infused with every form of Beauty

"Awakening should never be a dirge,"
you would say,
"But always an ecstatic dance
Joyfully finding our true rhythm
and living it passionately."

— DR. ANNE MCMURTRY —

KIRSTIN

Like the warmth of fire
Her goodness draws you into her heart
Where there is so much
Light and Peace

She can do a multitude of tasks
Because she never works alone
There is always a host of angels hovering around her
Sometimes you can even catch a glimpse of their wings
hovering on the edge of her flame

Like the sun that emits light equally
to the just and to the unjust
her generosity knows no bounds
yet often this generosity draws in souls
that steal her light
And so God sends her more of his guardians.
Like the angels who guarded Daniel in the fiery furnace
To keep her safe
and always in His Care.

MOTHE

Like blending wet and dry ingredients
when baking a cake
he blends the spiritual into the everyday
the timeless into each moment.

"These two realms are never separate,"
he would say,
"They are constantly intertwining and dancing
One into the Other."

The miraculous lies hidden within the ordinary
The key to opening this mystery
lies always within the heart
It knows there is no such duality
There is only Light and Love.

— DR. ANNE MCMURTRY —

BOB

Like the Dalai Lama
who said kindness was his religion
Bob likes to keep it simple
and always comes from his heart

He can sense what is needed before you tell him
and goes about doing it
drawing no attention to himself

He also realizes that if you don't break the rules
Now and then
Life has no spark
"Life is difficult enough as it is,"
he would say
"Let's have some fun!"

As a little child knows,
fun does not have to be complicated
It can be very simple
Like having enough marbles in your pocket to play with
when the relatives come to call.

Bob knows
that if you dwell in your heart
No matter how dark the moment
You can always find your way back to the Light.

JEAN

After being subjected to every form of suffering
You arrive at that turning point
where no horror can move you out of your heart
and where no suffering can cause you
to forget who you are.

Like Martin Luther, who said
"Here I stand. I will not be moved."
Today you have arrived at that point
Where a final refuge can be found
Where Peace can never be lost again

By seeing all of this horror
through the lens of Infinite Intelligence
and within the blazing fire
of God's Unconditional Love
You, like Job,
receive instantaneous healing
Not only the root of every disease
But the pain that was living in your heart.
The final piece, as you know, is the most challenging.
Where you will say
As Christ said
"Forgive them Father, for they know not what they do."

This propels your soul
Into eternal freedom
That clear white light
at the end of the tunnel.

— Dr. Anne McMurtry —

CHRISTINA

Like the Bodhisattva
Who postpones her final Enlightenment
until all sentient beings have been released from suffering
so you would gladly postpone you own entry
into the Final Bliss
until you have assisted all of God's creatures
in their journey from darkness to light
from suffering to Peace

Like Francis of Assisi
your most beloved companions
were often birds and animals
You never saw them as inferior to humans
but as some of God's most beloved friends
and most courageous angels

for your heart is a sacred space
where all beings can find love and healing

The challenge for you is always
to recognize God's signature
passionately inscribed
in your own heart.

KEN

In a world full of treachery
your energy is clean and clear
Like sunlight and mountain air
And your heart provides a refuge
A port in the storm, an oasis in the desert

But your greatest desire
is to be utterly transparent
Like Light itself
To have no barrier
between you
and the Infinite
Like a priest holding the sacraments
To embody the hands
and heart
of Christ.

— DR. ANNE MCMURTRY —

6

PATHWAYS

One light, light that is one though the lamps be many.

- DOUGLAS TRAHERNE HARDING

A Sacred Invitation

Dare I surrender to this ancient longing
with no language and no boundaries?
Dare I flow with this ageless love
that claims me
like a lover or a lost friend?

What a great light it sheds
in the cold grey night
And what a vast space it creates
in my heart!

With trembling hands, I light the flame
Which once lit can never be extinguished.

THE SIDDHA MASTERS

The Siddha Masters
are masters of that inner fire
that awakens
the Sacred Power within

Once that connection is made,
they continue to journey with us
Even into the realm of death.

Like the finest quality diamond,
their touch pierces us to the core
and compels us to make those changes
that will birth our true soul's purpose

To commit to walk with them,
Is not a light thing
Even though Light is their essence,

For it forges a sacred contract with spirit
That will last forever.

Often their greatest gift
is to free us from fear
so that we can uncover the God
within us
and allow Grace
to guide every area of our life.

— DR. ANNE MCMURTRY —

A True Master

Occasionally one meets a soul
that lights up the darkness
like an unflickering candle
Whose intention aligns with the angels
Whose heart emits a heavenly elixir
that soothes even the most weary soul.

Because their will is obedient to Divine Will
Even their physical presence shimmers with light
And the vibration of their voice is like sweet music.

Whenever such an invitation arises
to meet such a soul,
Never decline it
For an angel is knocking at your door.

NITYANANDA: THE JEWEL OF THE HEART

His Being emitted a deep indigo blue
as he came from the Unseen Realm of the Siddhas
His Silence was unfathomable
like the deepest depth of the ocean
Awakening in you a profound distaste for mere words and
ideas
Implanting instead an infinite yearning
For the things of the Heart

His Actions were often mysterious
yet conveyed great wisdom
for those who could decode their meaning
Children and animals flocked to him
as they felt the sweetness of his Presence

And like the scent of jasmine
His Goodness often emitted a subtle fragrance
He was a rare jewel
that continues to shimmer
in all of the Unseen Realms
and in the hearts of countless souls.

— DR. ANNE McMURTRY —

THE ALCHEMIST

How you have worked on this piece of coal
With the patient diligence
of Love
the power of Prayer
and with all the alchemy of Light
Until it begins to shine like a rainbow
Arching through the rain

And soon the diamond that you really are
begins to emerge
facet by facet
Each one shimmering
in a different way
in a kaleidoscope of colour

Now it's time to find just the right setting
for this precious stone
so that all its facets can unfold
like the petals of a rose
and the spirit within you
can finally find its wings.

LOVE IS A FORCE

Some say love is comfortable
like an old shoe
or a soft bed

I say love
Is a force which propels us
out of ourselves
and out of the known
Ecstatically
Like a volcano erupting

And we are tossed fearlessly
Into a totally new moment

As in the beginning
When we were spewed
Out of the Mother's Mouth
Like a million sparks of Light.

— DR. ANNE MCMURTRY —

AGAINST THE ASCETIC

Don't bandage me in your remote realm
That is bloodless and foreign to man's fever

I must drink from my tears
And build with my burdens
For my wings were fashioned
                    from the shadows

My wings must be weathered
By the dust that is driven
                    by a naked burning light.

I won't wander with your flesh
That freezes like the grave
Remote from the razor of time and desire
And man's raw despair.

MEDITATION

Meditation is not like freezing the mind
So that it doesn't move
Like a snapshot.

It is more like becoming
the lens of the camera itself
which views the constant flux
                        of the moment
from a state of still knowing.

For there is a lens within us
that witnesses every moment
without attachment
and without fear.

— DR. ANNE MCMURTRY —

A CONSOLATION

Dying is waking to see
That one has never been
      and never seen
and being walled into that shame
      that is weary now
As the womb

Seeing is but dying
Into that Deed
      That has always been
      And has always seen

And will never be weary

Even in the tomb.

Reiki

What is Reiki?

A sacred mystery in tangible form
An energy not of our making
                    that can flow through us
To heal broken bones, bruised hearts
And shattered lives.

It restores us
To that Divine Imprint
That ignites our soul's purpose
And fuels its sacred resolve.

It is a touch
That is both human and Divine

A healing bridge
That connects heaven and earth

It is a very safe way of going home.

— Dr. Anne McMurtry —

CHRISTOPHER REEVE: A SUPERMAN IN EVERY SENSE

The true Superman is not so much the hero
who defies gravity
flying like an eagle
to rescue stranded souls
on the highest building
but the man who defies despair
as he faces formidable human challenges
with courage and creativity

His wings are not so much part of a costume
but real extensions of his soul
taking him into that permanent realm of Light and Love
that awaits him on the other side.

He will never be forgotten.

THE LILY

The lily offers
        No solution
Merely ecstasy

— DR. ANNE MCMURTRY —

NATURE —THE SUPREME POETESS

We can learn so much from nature
Whose rhymes are always different
Whose images are always new
Like freshly baked bread

The Supreme Poetess continually destroying
and recreating Herself
in that Primal Fire

Even her lovemaking,
The way the sun embraces the sky
Or the wind caresses the leaves
And most especially the way the Light penetrates
Deeply into the heart of all beings,
Changes every moment.

No Kama Sutra could ever have foreseen
Such an abundance of sweet possibilities

Truly we are embraced every moment
by her infinite tenderness.

WE ARE "NOT"... EXCEPT THAT WE ARE HUNGRY

What child would ever play
With "that" doll?

And yet we still pretend to be.

How strange that beggars have such daring.

But then our hunger is no dream.
And only that will dress the doll
For the last pageant.

— DR. ANNE MCMURTRY —

ACKNOWLEDGMENTS

Let me begin by acknowledging the Divine Presence in my life that is forever inspiring me to be all that I can be.

In attempting to do so, I feel such gratitude for the loving support of my family. My father always had faith in me and recognized who I really was, even before I did. My mother was a constant source of comfort, especially during difficult times. Whatever she cooked for me was not only delicious, but infused with so much love. Even after her untimely death at age 27, the loving presence of my sister Jill has continued to journey with me and to inspire me with her courage and her outrageous humour. My brother Peter seems to have inherited our father's sense of humour and has been a real advocate for me. His two children, Lucy and Sarah, are extraordinary in all that they have accomplished – everything they do they do with real love. I also pay tribute to my sister-in-law, Susan, an incredible wife and mother who has reached out to me in so many ways.

My grandparents, Lois and Shirley McMurtry, lived life passionately and had great love and acceptance for every person they met. My grandmother on my mother's side spoiled us all with her amazing cooking!

My first cousins Nancy, Mary, and David have always supported me in all of my endeavours. It has seemed to me that their family and mine are really one indivisible family. We shared so much together in good, as well as difficult times. Their mother, my Aunt Marjorie, had the ability to listen to me from a very deep place of empathy. She too was a seeker.

I have been truly blessed with extraordinary friends whose unconditional love and encouragement have been a real anchor for me. It could be said that they are my second family, my "soul family." As Shakespeare said, "Those friends thou hast and their adoption tried, Grapple them to thy soul with hoops of steel." Devrah Laval has known and sustained me for lifetimes; our soul recognition has always been evident. Kathy France is another fortifying soul whose incomparable companionship I have known since time immemorial. Bernice Rochelle is also a dear friend who has carried me through myriad challenges, especially during the onset of menopause when she quite literally kept me on the planet. And Vedic astrologer Shanti Supernant's loving presence has helped me see more clearly the karmic patterns of my life.

Anne Leader has been a close friend over the years; her home-cooked meals have been a true delight. And Dee Willock was a stalwart source of strength at the time of my surgery. Barbara Halcrow has become an invaluable friend, giving me the necessary push to get this book published; I have "debriefed" with her many times, which has been invariably helpful. And I have been fortunate to know Pauline O'Reilly, who has listened to me with great attention and a big heart.

I extend my thanks to Karim Amersi and Joy Juenenann for being a sweet source of strength, and to my beloved friend, Stephen Kovacs, who has had my back in the most loving possible way. And to have been graced by the presence of Amanda Girin, Pratibha Saini, and Michaelyna Burianyk ("Miki") in my life has been a true blessing.

It is with the deepest appreciation that I acknowledge my many teachers. Carell Farmer's profound wisdom and loving support have guided me throughout my life, most especially during the difficult times. She has never failed to remind me that the most profound teacher is the teacher within. Ross Andaloro has also been a guiding light for me, illuminating many key issues in my life. And my paternal grandfather, one of my first spiritual teachers, shared with me much of his inner life and taught me to live from the heart. As Antoine de St. Exupery said, "It is only with the heart that one can see clearly. What is essential is invisible to the eye."

— Dr. Anne McMurtry —

Many of the souls who have been teachers for me are writers whom I have met on the inner planes, particularly Thomas Merton, R. M. Rilke, and Rabindrahath Tagore.

Reading Rilke's poetry taught me to chisel down each of my poems to the core, to remove anything inessential. As the great mystic, Meister Eckhart , has said, "Only the hand that erases can write the true thing."

Tagore was such a prolific poet that he even wrote a poem an hour before his death. In this excerpt, he describes the profound paradox of his life:
This way, radiant with a simple faith.
Tortuous it may be outwardly, but inwardly it is straight—
Herein is its glory.

I also want to acknowledge Treasa O'Driscoll, a Celtic poet and performer who has been a wonderful muse for me. She always urged me to keep writing these poems and even arranged for me to perform them at her home when she was living in Vancouver.

I am so blessed to have received editing support from Donaleen Saul, an author whose writing is impeccable and heartfelt. She and I have been friends over the years; we became especially close after the passing of her brother, Stephen. Donaleen connected me with Carol Sill, who is helping me on so many levels in finally publishing this book. Although we have only met recently, I have indeed known Carol of old. She is also a soul who truly comes from her heart.

There are so many souls who have helped me on this journey. You know who you are. I can't name all of you as the list would be too long, nor can I offer you sufficient thanks as I would speak of nothing else.

- *Dr. Anne McMurtry, Vancouver, 2020*

About the Author

Dr. Anne McMurtry has always been a spiritual seeker – a soul who has grappled with those questions that the Buddha deemed unanswerable. Rilke, the German poet, advised us to live out such questions until we are able, at some point in the future, to abide with the answers.

Two of these arose in Anne's life as a young woman: "Why did my sister, Jill, a young, gifted 27-year-old, die of cancer at such a young age? Why is there so much suffering and injustice in the world? Like Jacob wrestling with the angel, such questioning initiated and informed her lifelong spiritual quest.

As a young teenager, Anne bonded deeply with her grandfather, who often shared with her his unanswered questions, and with whom she frequently discussed theological and metaphysical matters. He spoke about having been sent to China as a physician, where he worked with the missionaries and experienced a dramatic clash of beliefs. He told the missionaries that he had the funds to open up a new hospital in China. Instead of encouraging him, they said: "You are here to save souls, not to worry about a new hospital!" He replied: "If someone is sick and I don't help them get well, or if they are hungry and I don't help them find food, then I know nothing of Christ. My work should never be about forcing my ideas and beliefs down someone's throat – it should always be about love."

This conversation with her grandfather made Anne realize the danger of any form of fundamentalism. This was reinforced, years later, when she was contemplating attaining a divinity degree at the University of McGill. There, she overheard two students saying, "Those poor Hindus and Buddhists are so lost. Isn't it great that we aren't following their path?" She was so outraged by this that she decided instead to get a Masters of Arts in Comparative Religion at the University of Lancaster in England. There she studied with the great scholar, Ninian Smart, a pioneer in the field of secular religious studies.

Subsequently, she entered a PhD program in Comparative Religion at McMaster University. There she worked with great scholars and spiritual adepts such as T.R.V. Murti, and her thesis supervisor, Dr. Maruthvar K. Sivaraman. She also received a Shastri-Indo-Canadian scholarship to spend a year in India working on her thesis. There, she had the privilege of meeting some of the greatest enlightened souls on the planet – including Krishnamurti, Anandamayi Ma, and Yogi Ramsuratkumar. She also spent time at a number of prominent ashrams, including those of Ramana Maharishi, Sivananda, and Aurobindo. She spent a whole week with Shri Ram Chandra, her first Master, at his home in Lucknow, sharing meals with him, discussing with him such questions such as "I already have a Master in Christ. Why do I need you as a Master?" His response was, "By working with me, you will be able to commune with Christ more deeply." Indeed, she frequently meditated with him in the sacred room he had dedicated to his Master, Lalaji Maharaj.

After completing her doctorate at McMaster University, Anne went on to teach for several years at the University of British Columbia in Vancouver. The students taking her World Religions course would attest that she encouraged them to grapple with the sacred teachings existentially by asking themselves the two fundamental life questions – "Who am I?" and "What is Real?" They would then go on to examine how the Hindu and Buddhist teachings, for example, addressed these inquiries quite differently.

Anne's teaching work was followed by a deeper calling – to work with sacred energies. This was facilitated by the passing of her sister, Jill, which seemed to open up a multidimensional portal, enabling her to speak with departed souls as well as with angels and personal guides. This new vocation was further reinforced by a meeting with a healer in San Francisco, who told her that her academic work was just a small part of her destiny and that her real work was about to begin. Heeding this powerful message, Anne immediately began working with quartz crystals and the sacred energy, Reiki. Having done such work in several past lives, this was a deeply familiar path for her.

In 2004 she was ordained in the Spiritus Ministry by Bishop Glenda Green, D.D., who is an artist and channel herself.

In her healing work, Anne helps her clients remove the obstacles that prevent them from experiencing their essence and moving forward with their life's purpose. It often involves helping them discover the spiritual practice that's right for them. She firmly believes in never pushing any of them in a spiritual direction that isn't right for them. To validate this intention, Anne finds inspiration in this passage from the *Bhagavad-Gita*: "Better is one's own svadharma (path), though badly performed, than the path of someone else well-performed.

Although Anne had been writing poetry since age 21, it was when she shifted to working with energies that poetry became a more prominent part of her life. Once she began working as a channel, her poetry moved to a new level; she experienced poems coming to her in much the same way as she received messages from the other side when doing readings with clients.

Many of her poems to individuals could be characterized as celebrating and expressing each person's uniqueness. Getting out of the way and letting Spirit speak is a central intention of her poetry practice. She acknowledges the poems as gifts from Spirit, although she certainly admits to being part of the process!

With respect to both her work as a healer and as a poet, Anne has been known to say, "If my work seems like work, it won't work; if it seems like play, it always works."

Anne's next step is offering a yearlong seminar and workshop on angels. She feels that it is especially important to work with them at this critical time in our species' and our planet's evolution.

Made in the USA
Columbia, SC
17 August 2020